SUPER STRUCTURES OF THE WORLD

THE LONDON UNDERGROUND

BLACKBIRCH®
PRESS

THOMSON
™
GALE

San Diego • Detroit • New York • San Francisco • Cleveland • New Haven, Conn. • Waterville, Maine • London • Munich

THOMSON

GALE

LIBRARY OF CONGRESS CATALOGING-IN-PUBLICATION DATA

London underground / Elaine Pascoe, book editor.
    p. cm. — (Super structures of the world)
Summary: Examines the history of London's subway system, known as the Tube, including some of the challenges faced in design and construction and its uses during World War II. Includes bibliographical references and index.
  ISBN 1-56711-866-6 — ISBN 1-4103-0190-7
  1. Subway stations—England—London—Juvenile literature. 2. Subways—England—London—Design and construction—Juvenile literature. [1. Subways—England—London.] I. Pascoe, Elaine. II. Series.

  TF847.L6L66 2004
  388.4'28'09421—dc21   2003007519

THE LONDON UNDERGROUND

Above ground, it seems like just another day in London. But sixty feet down, beneath the historic streets, is one of Europe's most massive engineering projects.

An army of twenty thousand people worked six years to build this $4.5-billion project. It's the Jubilee Line Extension to the London Underground, the world's oldest and greatest subway, otherwise known as the Tube or the "train in the drain."

Above: It took a construction crew six years to build the Jubilee Line Extension to the London Underground. This historic subway is the main source of London's public transportation.

EUSTON ALDWYCH CITY PAR·
SQ

London is an ancient city. When the Romans arrived more than two thousand years ago, there was already a settlement here. Over the centuries, it's been ruled by countless kings and queens. It is here that Shakespeare wrote his plays and modern democracy was born.

But London today works thanks to something invented 150 years ago and improved constantly since—the Tube. The subway runs through the city the way arteries run through a body, keeping it alive.

The London subway has a simple mission: Move a great number of people efficiently, quickly, and safely. Some 800 million travelers use the system every year. Above ground, the streets grow more and more congested.

Top left: The 800 million people who travel through London each year congest the city's streets. Top right: London is full of history. The Tube, invented more than 150 years ago, is just one part of the ancient city's history.

The Jubilee Line Extension is the first new subway project in London for twenty years. It added ten miles of new tunnels and gave travelers access to areas of London never served by the Tube before. The project was finished in December 2000, just in time to carry fifty thoudsand passengers an hour to the Millennium Dome, built for London's huge millennium celebration.

Many of the engineers for this project were seasoned veterans of the Channel Tunnel, the thirty-one-mile undersea link between England and France. But the Jubilee Line presented these veteran engineers with a greater technical challenge than the Chunnel.

Above left: The Jubilee Line Extension was finished in 2000, and was the first new subway project in twenty years.

Left: Many Jubilee Line engineers had also worked on the Channel Tunnel, the transportation system underneath the ocean that connects England and France.

LONDON'S CHALLENGE

The Jubilee Line tunnels had to be carefully threaded through an already overcrowded subterranean city, packed with older Tube lines and a spaghetti of sewer lines, water mains, gas mains, and cables. The waterlogged soils near the Thames River threatened to collapse during construction. The engineers had at their disposal the latest tunneling technologies. But they were on a tight timetable, and there was no margin for error.

Above: Engineers mapped the tunnels for the Jubilee Line around other Tube lines already in existence, as well as sewer lines and water mains.

Right: During construction of the London Underground, engineers feared that the waterlogged soil near the Thames River would collapse.

One of the prime concerns for the extension was tunneling beneath Westminster, site of the British Houses of Parliament and Big Ben. Big Ben may be an international landmark, but its Victorian builders gave it poor supports. And two new Jubilee Line tunnels pass a mere twenty meters from the building's frail foundations.

The weak supports of Big Ben (top) and the British House of Parliament (above right) concerned tunnel engineers, who had to construct tunnels (above left) under the landmarks.

The bane of all tunnelers is subsidence—the tendency of ground above a tunnel to sink. To check for subsidence, the engineers clamped some seven thousand electronic monitoring points to the historic and not-so-historic buildings surrounding the Westminster area. The sensitive monitors would instantly detect any movement.

Above: Engineers used electric monitoring systems to detect subsidence, or the tendency of ground above a tunnel to sink.

Detecting subsidence is one thing. Preventing it is another. So engineers came up with a sophisticated technical fix—permeation grouting.

Right: Positioned in the Westminster area of London, monitors could detect even the slightest movement and alert engineers of subsidence.

Left: Injection tubes, spread under at-risk buildings like Big Ben, kept the structures stationary.

Right: Permeation grouting injects concrete into the ground above dig sites. This system keeps the soil immobile and does not allow it to shift.

This process calls for injecting concrete into the ground above the dig sites, to keep the soil from shifting. First, large main shafts were dug. From these shafts, smaller injection tubes spread out under the buildings most at risk. Into these shafts and tributaries, the cement was carefully injected. The engineers' precision achieved the necessary stability, and Big Ben stands as straight and tall today as it has for 150 years.

The difficulties faced by the Jubilee Line engineers and their ability to devise imaginative solutions are an integral part of the London subway's proud engineering tradition, a tradition stretching back to its very beginning.

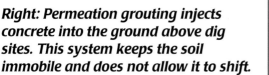

THE FIRST SUBWAY

In 1850 London was the world's largest city and the most congested. Two and a half million people were crammed into sixty square miles. The city was crowded, filthy, and filled with horses and carts. The only roads were a network of narrow streets designed centuries earlier.

Something had to be done.

Outside London, there was an impressive system of railroads. But trains were not allowed into the town itself. It took the vision of Charles Pearson, solicitor to the City of London, to devise the bold solution: Put the railroads underground.

Above Left: With a population of 2.5 million people, London was the largest city in the world in 1850.

Left: Because trains and railroads were not allowed inside London, city solicitor Charles Pearson developed a new plan.

Engineers chose a simple method—cut and cover—to build the first subway, the Metropolitan Line. They dug big trenches, laid tracks, and then roofed them over. But another challenge confronted the engineers: The train engines were steam powered. In the confined tunnels, the engines' toxic fumes would poison passengers.

Above: For the cut-and-cover method, workers dug big trenches, laid tracks, and then installed roofing over them.

Below: Steam-powered trains emitted fumes that, if confined in an underground system, could poison passengers.

Above: Engineers used a cut-and-cover method to build the first underground railroad—or subway—the Metropolitan Line.

The solution was the condensing engine—a steam engine that piped its exhaust into two huge holding tanks on its side. The holding tanks quickly filled up with fumes, so engineers had to find ways to empty them. You can see their ingenious solution today at 23–24 Leinster Gardens in London's Paddington district. To the casual observer, these houses are like any other on the street. But the windows are false and there are no mailboxes. It is only from above that one can see the real purpose of these fake houses. They cleverly hide subway vent holes, where the engine's holding tanks could be cleared safely.

The Metropolitan Line ran for three and a half miles between Paddington and Farringdon in the city. It was an immediate success.

But the cut-and-cover method was enormously disruptive. It required digging up main streets to build the tunnels—an approach that only added to the congestion of London. If the subway was to expand, a less disruptive method of construction was needed.

Above: Engineers created a condensing engine to solve the steam train problem. These new trains piped exhaust into holding tanks instead of releasing it into the air, which would have been poisonous. This spread: Construction crews built the Metropolitan Line to cover three and a half miles under the streets of London.

DIGGING DEEPER

The answer was to dig deeper, tunneling below the city. But tunneling through the waterlogged soil below London presented a huge challenge.

The man who first devised a technique for tunneling in waterlogged soil was Marc Isambard Brunel, a celebrated British engineer. He built the first major canal in America, the Lake Champlain-Hudson Waterway. In 1825 he started work on a tunnel for pedestrians under the Thames.

Right: Engineer Marc Isambard Brunel invented a system to build tunnels through waterlogged soil, a previously unfathomable feat.

Left: Before working on the Underground, Brunel designed a pedestrian tunnel to run under the Thames River.

To solve the problem of the soft mud below the river, Brunel devised a huge rectangular shield. It provided a solid roof over the heads of workers, to protect them as they clawed their way through the earth. Still, during construction there were two collapses, and ten people drowned. But after fifteen years, the five-hundred-yard-long tunnel was completed.

Top: Brunel created a huge rectangular shield to protect workers as they plowed through the earth.

Above: It took fifteen years to complete construction of the five-hundred-yard-long tunnel.

Above: This drawing depicts a collapse during underground construction, where ten people drowned.

In 1880 plans were made for a new pedestrian tunnel beneath the Thames. The engineer, James Henry Greathead, improved on Brunel's design. His tunneling machine was smaller and lighter than Brunel's. And, most importantly, it was circular in shape, giving the tunnel the optimum shape for strength.

Above: James Henry Greathead improved Brunel's design by making the new pedestrian tunnel round. Greathead also invented a smaller, lighter tunneling machine.

Greathead also designed the machine so that as the earth was removed, hydraulic rams pushed it forward. Workers behind the machine would then bolt cast-iron lining sections into place, securing the tunnel. Finally, cement would be pumped into the area between the iron lining and the surrounding earth, ensuring a tight and waterproof fit. It was a painstaking process, resulting in only five feet of tunnel every twelve hours.

Greathead's new tunneling machine would allow the subway, for the first time, to be dug deep beneath the city. Construction could go on without disrupting traffic above. In 1886 Greathead, with his digging machines, set to work constructing an additional four miles of tunnels, linking King William Street with Stockwell.

Left: Greathead's invention pushed the earthen soil forward as it was removed.

Above: Cement was pumped into the space between the earth and the iron lining, a sluggish but important part of the new construction plan.

Left: For the first time, the subway could be constructed deep underneath London and not affect life aboveground.

But now the subway had another problem: Steam engines were useless in the deeper tunnels because there was nowhere to vent their deadly fumes. Newly developed electric engines provided the answer. To this day, London's Tube trains are powered by electricity, with the design changing little over one hundred years. Each line has four rails, two for wheels and two live rails that carry 630 volts of electricity. The current is picked up from the live rails by shoes on the train, powering the electric motors.

The first electric engines were used in the subway in 1890. They were British-built and pulled three cars. For the early passengers, who considered gaslights in the street exotic, the subway was a fantastical voyage into the future.

Above: In 1890 the Tube used its first electric engines. These engines only pulled three cars.

Right: Passengers in the 1890s considered the Tube a futuristic accomplishment.

This page: The lines of today's London subway, like those of the past one hundred years, are electrically powered. Two of each line's four rails carry 630 volts of electricity.

YANKEE INGENUITY

With deep tunneling techniques and electric locomotion, the stage was set for the subway to expand. But where would London get the money to electrify the lines and dig the new tunnels?

It would come from Charles Tyson Yerkes, a financier from Chicago who had made his fortune on tramcars. This go-getting American was to become the driving force behind the great expansion of London's subways at the turn of the century.

Left: Chicago financier Charles Tyson Yerkes financed the first expansion of the London Underground.

Right: Yerkes built the world's largest power station in Chelsea. This station could produce more than 180 megawatts of electricity at one time.

Left: Steam turbines generated electricity at the Chelsea power plant, which powered the London Underground for nearly a century.

Yerkes bought up the various competing lines and then set about electrifying them. At Chelsea, he built the world's largest power station. When it opened in 1905, the Lots Road plant was called "the Chelsea monster." The plant used a new technology for generating electricity, steam turbines, and it stood the test of time. The Chelsea monster powered the London subways for almost a century. At peak times, it produced more than 180 megawatts of electricity, enough to light a small city.

Right: Today escalators carry passengers from the subway to the streets above. Early passengers, however, were distrustful of the first escalator's safety.

Above: While engineers originally tried to use elevators at subway stations, they quickly discovered a better solution—the American escalator.

With the subway tunnels now as much as one hundred feet below street level, it was inconvenient for passengers to go up and down endless flights of stairs. Yerkes' first solution was to use elevators, but they were soon overwhelmed. The solution proved to be an American invention, the escalator. Today there are more than four hunderd escalators in the London Underground. But when the first escalator was installed in 1911, it was not immediately popular. The company hired a man with a wooden leg to ride up and down all day, to reassure the passengers of its safety.

The American influence on London's Underground went further than financing and technical solutions. In Britain, trains are made up of "carriages"; only on the Tube is a train carriage called a "car." Other

Americanisms seeped in, too. Subway trains are "northbound" and "southbound" instead of the traditional British "up" and "down." Even "OK" is part of the subway lingo.

Above: There are now more than four hundred escalators in subway stations across London.

Right: American influence changed the wording on subway signs from "up" and "down" to "northbound" and "southbound."

The cost of building and powering deep-level subways was enormous, $28 million a mile in today's money. To justify such an investment, the London subway needed more revenue. The solution was to expand the network out from central London into the suburbs. And once the trains were in place, the new riders built their houses near the stations.

At the same time, the subway tried to entice travelers to come back into the city. Posters tempted people to London's West End at night. Traveling by Tube was as much part of the evening out as seeing a film or play.

But soon enough, Londoners were to get a very different sort of nightlife, and the Underground would play a major new role.

Left: The ballrooms and theaters of London's West End drew revelers who considered the ride on the Tube part of the night's festivities.

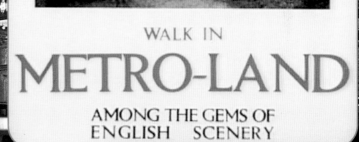

WALK IN

METRO-LAND

AMONG THE GEMS OF
ENGLISH SCENERY

Above: As more and more people moved out of the suburbs, posters tempted them to ride the subway back into London.

Left: Travel by Tube became a major part of an evening out—as much as going to an event such as the circus.

CIRCUS

go by
Underground

THE TUBE IN WORLD WAR II

World War II hit London hard. Between August 1940 and July 1941, German planes dropped more than forty thousand high explosives and millions of incendiary devices on London. The assault was known as the Blitz. By the end, thirty-two thousand men, women, and children were dead and 30 percent of the city was in ruins.

Right: The Blitz, a German military assault on London during World War II, killed more than thirty-two thousand people and destroyed 30 percent of the city.

Left: More than forty thousand explosives were dropped on London during the assault in 1940 and 1941.

There were few bomb shelters in the early days of World War II, so in desperation Londoners turned to the Tube. Because of their depth, the tunnels offered shelter from the inferno above. At first, British authorities tried to keep the people out, maintaining that they would prevent the system from running efficiently. Londoners simply ignored the ban and bought tickets, camping out on platforms, in passageways, and even on the escalators.

Above: Because the city had few bomb shelters, Londoners escaped the bombs to the tunnels of the Underground.

Right: London citizens disregarded the ban that prohibited staying in the Underground. Instead, they camped out everywhere, even on the escalators.

Accepting reality, the subway authorities came up with ways to serve overnight visitors. Some trains were converted to Tube Refreshment Specials, providing hot chocolate and buns for everyone. London had gone underground.

For people like seventy-eight-year-old Joyce Morrell, time has not faded memories of those long nights in the tunnels. "We all tried to help one another, looking after the children or trying to soothe them down, trying

Left: Some trains were changed into Tube Refreshment Specials and became underground coffeehouses.

Right: Joyce Morrell, a one-time tube dweller, remembers using the Underground as a shelter during World War II.

JOYCE MORRELL
TUBE SHELTERER 1940-41

Left: The Tube Refreshment Specials, trains that were converted to serve food and drink, offered hot chocolate and buns to those hiding in the tunnels.

Right: Some Underground tunnels became temporary factories that built aircraft parts needed by Britain's Royal Air Force.

to help the people who were feeling very panic-stricken. One didn't really have time to think of one-self," she recalls. "But of course the following morning, we didn't know whether we were going to find our houses still standing or not."

Some of the tunnels were converted into factories. One housed two thousand workers who built aircraft parts for Royal Air Force planes. Another became an improvised art gallery, protecting the precious treasures of the British Museum from the Nazi bombs.

This page: The Thames and the station entrances potentially endangered those who lived in the Underground. If a bomb exploded in the Thames and ruptured a tunnel, river water could flood the entire Underground.

As a shelter, the Underground had two strategic weak points, the river and the station entrances. A bomb exploding in the Thames could rupture a tunnel under the river and flood the entire system. To prevent this, engineers installed huge floodgates on each end of tunnels running under the river. But little could be done to protect the many vulnerable station entrances. In 1941 a bomb bounced down into Bank Station, exploding on the escalator. Tragically, fifty-six Londoners lost their lives.

Above left: Londoners were forced to flee from bombs even while hiding out in the Tube. Top: Engineers built floodgates at each end of the underwater tunnels to prevent potential flooding. Above right: Fifty-six people died when a bomb bounced into Bank Station and exploded on an escalator.

SHELTERS

OLDHAM	NELSON
AND TO	AND TO
PARRY	MADDEN
MEDICAL AID POST	MEDICAL AID POST
CANTEEN	CANTEEN
LAVATORIES	LAVATORIES

Top left: Prime Minister Winston Churchill stepped in to protect London after a new Nazi campaign was unleashed in 1944. Above: Churchill's plan created eight new tunnels built to house citizens. Left: Hitler's new military campaign launched V-1 and V-2 rockets on London, which caused devastation to the city.

When the Blitz ended, Londoners joyously returned to the open air. But worse was to follow. In 1944 Hitler began a new campaign of terror, launching V-1 and V-2 rockets on the city, forcing Londoners back underground. This time, they had more choices. Prime Minister Winston Churchill had additional deep tunnels built, with the idea that after the war they would be used as subways.

In all, eight tunnels were built, and many survive to this day, although they were never integrated into the system. One tunnel is still used for government document storage. Another became the headquarters for General Eisenhower. In this tunnel, Ike and the Allied Command devised the plans for Operation Overlord, otherwise known as D day.

With V-E Day in 1945, the London subway could return to its former civilian purpose. During the six years of war, this Victorian super structure had saved thousands of lives from Nazi bombs. But the future would present new and deadlier threats.

Above: One of the former tunnel shelters is now used to store government documents.

Below: Another former tunnel is now the Eisenhower Centre, where General Dwight D. Eisenhower and the Allied Command conceived the plans for D day.

NEW DANGERS

Since 1990 the London Underground has received more than ten thousand terrorist alerts, an average of three a day. The confined, crowded stations are a perfect target. In the closed space of a subway, there is no escape from the blast and destructive power of a well-placed bomb.

For those responsible for the Tube's security, that threat demands constant vigilance.

"We have to deal with people who are determined in their goals to achieve major disruption and sometimes loss of life in the United Kingdom, but particularly in London," says Steve Hotston, chief of police for the London Underground. "And the Underground, as a target, is one which they've favored in the past."

CHIEF SUPT. STEVE HOTSTON
CHIEF OF POLICE, LONDON UNDERGROUND
POLICE

Above: The Underground received three terrorist alerts each day since 1990, keeping its security personnel busy.

Left: Underground police chief Steve Hotston takes the threats seriously and sees the Underground as the perfect target for terrorists.

This page: A carefully placed bomb could easily do serious damage to the crowded stations of the Tube.

Until recently, the prime terrorist concern was the IRA, the Irish Republican Army. Since 1972 the IRA has waged a sustained war of terror on Britain in its struggle to win a united Ireland. To fight the terrorists, London's subway police force has gone high tech.

The Tube's communications and surveillance center is a state-of-the-art facility. It provides authorities with instant access to nearly fifteen hundred video cameras. The cameras closely monitor all the comings and goings of the subway stations.

"If you enter the system anywhere on the Underground," says Hotston, "we can pick you up and follow you across the whole system."

Right: Key surveillance points line this map of the Underground, which uses a state-of-the-art system to monitor its security.

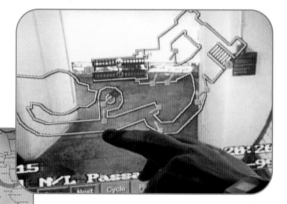

Left: Underground employees monitor the fifteen hundred surveillance cameras located around the subway stations.

As an added benefit, subway crime has fallen by 40 percent since the cameras went up. As a result, London has one of the safest subway systems in the world.

But things can still go wrong. And when they do, London's elite Underground Emergency Response Unit is trained to respond quickly. The unit can deal with any kind of catastrophe, from derailments to fires to bombings.

The unit was needed in February 1975, when a runaway train careened into the buffers at Moorgate Station. The cars were sandwiched, one literally on top of the other. In all, 42 people died and another 150 were seriously injured.

Top right: Surveillance cameras have helped reduce subway crime by 40 percent. Middle: The Underground Emergency Response Unit deals with all disasters at the Tube. Bottom: In 1975 a runaway train smashed into the buffers at Moorgate Station and killed forty-two people.

Left: A devastating fire, ignited by a dropped cigarette, broke out at King's Cross Station in 1987 and killed thirty-one people.

LONDON FIRE BRIGADE VIDEO

Right: Pushed into the King's Cross Station by moving trains, oxygen fueled the fire as workers rushed to put it out.

Twelve years later, tragedy struck yet again. At 7:30 P.M. on a brisk November evening, a terrible, all-consuming fire broke out at King's Cross Station, one of the system's busiest. The Underground Emergency Response Unit was called into action. Before it was over, thirty-one people were dead, all the result of a cigarette that had been innocently dropped on the station's old wooden escalator. The Tube itself contributed to the intensity of the blaze. Trains that continued to run pushed oxygen into the station, fueling the inferno.

The King's Cross fire resulted in massive safety changes. The wooden escalators were replaced, fire retardant materials were used in new station construction, and training and evacuation procedures greatly improved.

Right: The fire prompted officials to take a good look at the Underground's construction and assess the need for updates.

Left: New evacuation procedures are now in place as well as new station construction to meet safety conditions.

The fire brought home the fact that the main enemy of the Underground is its age. Much of the subway is more than one hundred years old and in dire need of a massive overhaul. Yet there is little time for upkeep, because the system runs twenty hours a day, seven days a week. Repairs can only be carried out during the four hours from 1:00 to 5:00 A.M. The loneliest overnight maintenance job is track walking— walking the tracks at night to carefully inspect the network.

A maintenance army of fifteen hundred men and women works against the clock to keep the London Underground running. But as the

system gets older, the repairs get more difficult. It's estimated that $16 billion is needed to bring the Underground up to date. It costs $400 million a year merely to repair and renew the current system. So when engineers got a chance to build a new line for the subway, they were determined to get it right.

Above right: Fifteen hundred people make up the Underground's maintenance crew. The crew works continuously to ensure the smooth operation of the Tube.

Right: The creation of a new and modern subway line could cost $16 billion.

BUILDING THE JUBILEE LINE

The Jubilee Line Extension was designed to ensure that tragedies like the fire at King's Cross or the accident at Moorgate never happen again. Engineers used the latest and most sophisticated technology to build the Jubilee's tunnels, trains, and stations.

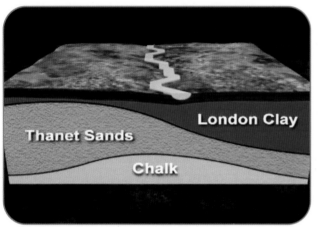

Above: This image shows the geology of London. The original subway tunnels wind through the clay area.

The extension also tackled one problem that engineers had mostly managed to avoid, the complex and challenging geology of London itself. London is split in two by the Thames River. The bulk of the Tube system was dug north of the river for one simple reason: The thick layer of clay on that side of the Thames is ideal to tunnel through. South of the Thames, the clay is much thinner. Just beneath the fine clay strata is porridge of water-bearing soils and gravels. Tunneling through these soils is like digging through a waterlogged beach.

The principle aid in building tunnels in waterlogged ground is compressed air. James Henry Greathead pioneered this technique, when he built the subway tunnels in the late nineteeth century. High-pressure air is pumped into a sealed chamber at the tunnel's face, keeping water away from the digging

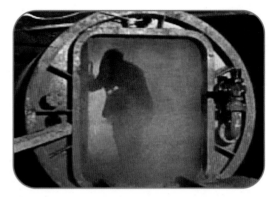

surface. Working in this environment can be risky—the high pressure necessary to hold water back is equivalent to being forty feet below sea level. If workers emerge from the airlock without going into a decompression chamber, they face the bends and possible death.

Top right: In order to keep water away from the construction area, Jubilee Line workers pump high-pressure air into a sealed chamber in the tunnel, which creates a potentially deadly work environment. Above: The new, revolutionary tunneling machines used in construction of the Jubilee Line allowed workers to remain in an environment with normal air pressure.

But the Jubilee Line used a new kind of tunneling machine. Only the very front of the machine, where the cutting blades are, was pressurized, so workers could to their job in an area with normal air pressure. In all, the Jubilee Line tunnels back and forth beneath the Thames four times.

The Jubilee tunneling machines operated on a massive scale. In the past, it would have taken dozens of men to do the work of these mechanical moles, with their enormous cutting blades. The monsters advanced slowly but relentlessly through the London clay. For each meter of tunnel dug, forty tons of earth was carried away on conveyors. As the machine moved forward, engineers put in place preformed concrete tunnel sections.

From time to time, the monster moles bumped up against London's past. At London Bridge, tunnelers found the debris from a Roman house, smothered by the unforgiving mud. At the new train depot at Stratford, a

burial ground for Cistercian monks was discovered. This was the site of a monastery built in 1134 and destroyed by Henry VIII in 1538. All told, archaeologists removed 678 skeletons for a respectful burial before work started up again.

Above: The current technology of the tunneling machines makes them powerful mechanical moles that can do the work of dozens of men.

Right: Tunnelers on the Jubilee Line project unearthed the remains of a Roman house near the tunnel site at London Bridge and a monk burial ground at Stratford.

A SUBWAY FOR THE FUTURE

The Jubilee Line's stations are designed to serve passengers safely for the next century. The new stations are enormous— the Canary Wharf Station, for instance, is larger than the massive sky-scraper that overshadows it. They're designed with safety in mind. Platform

edge doors line each platform, greatly reducing the wind effect that fed the flames at King's Cross. The doors also reduce access to the tracks. This will cut down on suicide attempts. Twice a week, someone falls or jumps onto the Underground's tracks.

Above: The Jubilee Line stations are huge, larger even than some skyscrapers.

Right: Doors that line the edges of station platforms reduce blustery winds that could feed potential fires and also serve as barriers to prevent suicide attempts.

The Jubilee Line has state–of–the–art trains and cars, fifty-nine automatic trains of six cars each. They run every two and a half minutes, moving fifty thousand passengers an hour. The trains are designed with crumple zones to absorb impact, addressing the problem that killed so many people in the Moorgate crash. Each train also has black-box incident recorders, similar to those on airplanes.

Right: The Jubilee Line's high-tech trains run on an automatic schedule and move fifty thousand passengers every hour.

Left: The new, modern trains have shock absorbers in the case of a crash and black box recorders, like those on airplanes.

The Jubilee Line ran over budget and way over schedule. Yet the engineers achieved their objective, building the most advanced subway system in the world. Now they are looking to the future. On the drawing board is a new type of subway train for London,

the Space Train. It will increase passenger capacity by over 40 percent without changing the size of London's narrow tunnels.

The London Underground has served its city well, providing efficient, safe transport in times of peace and protection in times of war. Today the train in the drain continues to be the world's leader in mass transportation, keeping its proud place as a super structure like no other.

Above: After a long six years, engineers and workers celebrated the completion of the Jubilee Line, the most advanced subway system in the world. Left: Engineers are already at work creating the next subway super structure—the Space Train.

GLOSSARY

airlock a chamber with two airtight doors between two different environments

bends a sometimes fatal condition caused by too rapid a decrease in air pressure after being in a compressed atmosphere

blitz the massive German aerial bombardment of London during World War II

condensing engine a steam engine that piped its exhaust into holding tanks for later release

engineer professionals who determine how to build something and oversee the process

hydraulic operated or moved by the use of liquids such as oil or water

IRA Irish Republican Army

operation overlord the Allied invasion of Normandy during World War II, also known as D day

permeation grouting injection of concrete into the ground to prevent it from shifting

steam turbine a rotary engine that is turned by the force of steam

subsidence the tendency of the ground above a tunnel to sink

subterranean below the ground

toxic poisonous

V-E Day The day that Germany surrendered in World War II, May 8, 1945

vigilance the quality or state of being alertly watchful

INDEX

DATE DUE

GAYLORD

PRINTED IN U.S.A.